BRAVE NEW BALLET

THE STORY OF LES BALLETS TROCKADERO DE MONTE CARLO

by Robyn McGrath

illustrated by
Alexander Mostov

PENGUIN WORKSHOP

PENGUIN WORKSHOP
An imprint of Penguin Random House LLC
1745 Broadway, New York, NY 10019
penguinrandomhouse.com

Design by Taylor Abatiell
Text set in Julius Primary Std

The art was created with pencil, paper, and Procreate. Plus lots of coffee.

Library of Congress Cataloging-in-Publication Data is available.

First published in the United States of America by Penguin Workshop, 2026

Manufactured in China
HH

ISBN 9798217049370
10 9 8 7 6 5 4 3 2 1

The authorized representative in the EU for product safety and compliance is Penguin Random House Ireland, Morrison Chambers, 32 Nassau Street, Dublin D02 YH68, Ireland, https://eu-contact.penguin.ie.

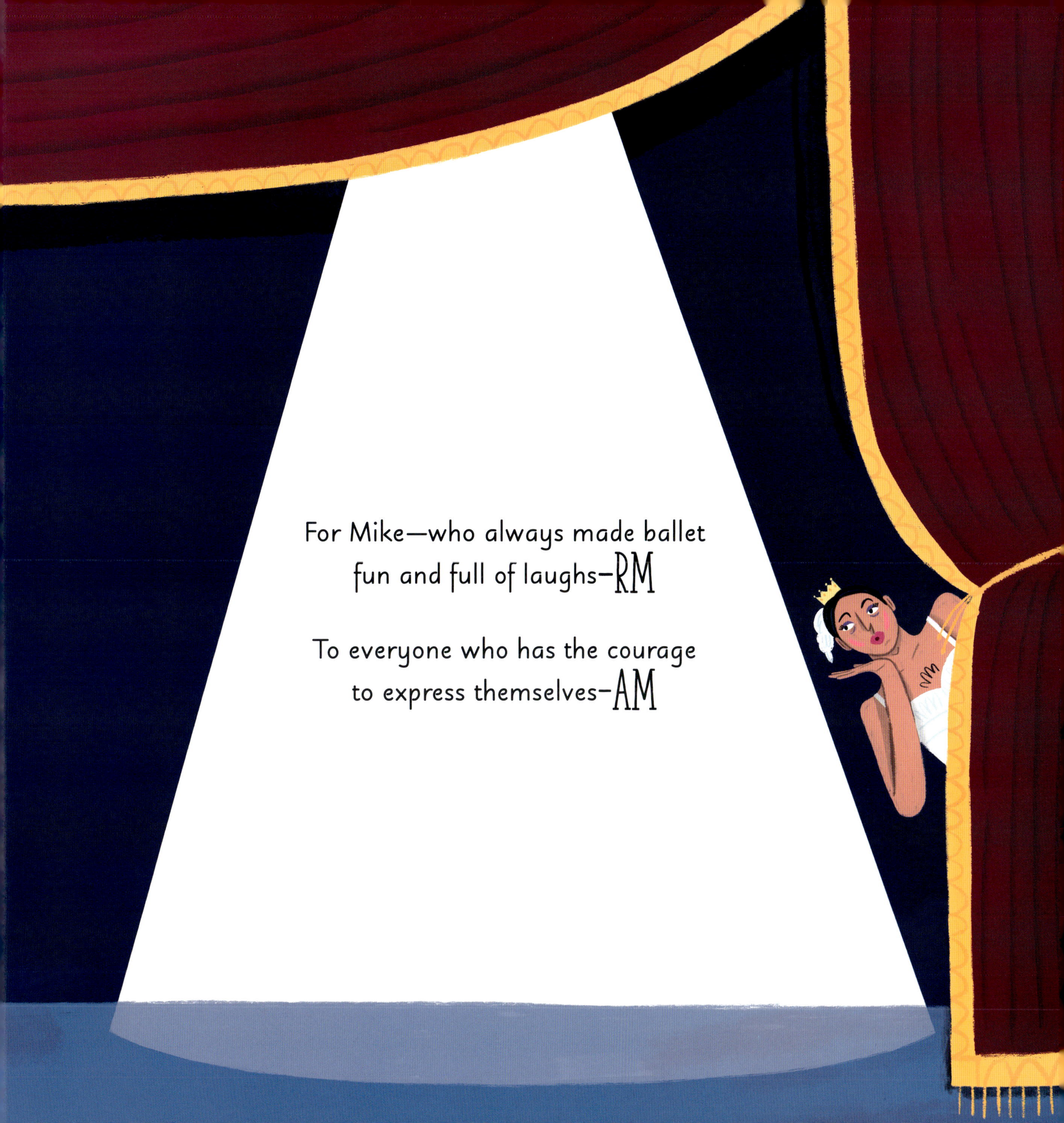

For Mike—who always made ballet fun and full of laughs–RM

To everyone who has the courage to express themselves–AM

They arrived in New York City
from around the world,
looking for their *BIG* break.

Their chance to dance on center stage,
under the bright lights,
to sold-out audiences.

It was the early 1970s,
a time of change . . .
when this brave group of dancers,
with a passion for ballet
and the courage to be themselves,
kicked through barriers to follow their dreams.

On the second floor of a run-down
warehouse building,
in the dark of night,

a ballerina practices.

PLIÉ

RELEVÉ

TENDU

Over and over.
Hour after hour.
A tutu wrapping their waist,
floating across the makeshift stage . . .

EN POINTE.

While traditional male dancers perform the role of the prince, and save the swan princess . . . this male dancer *is* the swan princess.

He is part of an all-male ballet troupe,

LES BALLETS TROCKADERO DE MONTE CARLO.

Pronounced:
TROCK-uh-dare-oh.
And oh yes, they dare to be different!

Together, these ballerinas aspire
to dance and have fun . . .
without restrictions!

Dancing the female roles means learning to dance ballet all over again.
It will not be easy—but they cannot wait to try!

Some Trockaderos, or Trocks for short, replace their soft black dancing slippers with rigid pink pointe shoes.

Like walking on stilts, they try to find their balance.

Blisters and ice.
Swollen toes and tape.

OUCH!

Sprained ankles,
torn ligaments,
and pulled hamstrings.

Every ounce of pain is worth it.
This feels like what they were born to do!
Each choreographed movement . . .
fills them with hope.

Can they leap out of the
shadows into the spotlight?

Training under demanding instructors, the men learn the classic Russian ballets—

SWAN LAKE,

LES SYLPHIDES,

and *DON QUIXOTE.*

Dancing both the male *AND* female roles . . .
they master the difficult movements.

And then amid the struggle, something surprising happens!

The Trocks make the classical ballets entirely their own.

The dancers in drag add a dash of unexpected humor to the choreography.

A *WINK*,

a *HIGH FIVE*,

or *A FUNNY GLARING LOOK*.

Still, these ballerinas are not taken seriously.

Men in heavy makeup,
wigs,
tutus,
and pointe shoes?

Reviewers and audiences turn away.

Chins up,
the Trocks hold true to what they believe in . . .
dancing to entertain while openly expressing themselves.

They continue to perform in the *late* late shows,
off-off-Broadway.

Each performance bolsters their courage to persist.
Balanced *en pointe*, they twirl across the floor.
Some shuffle flatfoot in *arabesque*.

Dancing freely, they add even more personality to their stage characters.

A raised eyebrow,

a sassy *CHASSÉ*,

or a flip of the wig.

And the audience?
Some erupt in laughter and applause.
Others walk out in a huff!

"How dare they?"

"So crude!"

Not everyone agrees they are a "real" ballet company.

But the Trocks are celebrating ballet, NOT making fun of it. These are dedicated dancers who dare to do something different.

They will not be beaten down by bad reviews or narrow minds!

Proving that they can do what they love,
the Trocks become more disciplined with each

PORT DE BRAS,

BATTEMENT,

and ATTITUDE.

REHEARSE,
PERFORM,
REPEAT.
Finally, one night,
enter . . .

. . . THE DYING SWAN.

Delicately balanced on his toes.
Feathers floating to the ground around him.
A long extension of his leg with perfectly pointed toes.
Giving the audience a side smile, suggesting,

"Did you see that?"

"Do you see me?"

Tightly executed *bourrées* end with an exasperated face.
And their *grand jetés* end with a shrug, "no big deal."
Precision, strength, technique,
and comedy.

The Trocks dance with emotion, confidence, and grace.

It is a breakthrough performance!

Their choreographed antics?

ON POINT!

Their dancing?

EXTRAORDINARY!

Soon word spreads around New York City.

Curious audiences become energized and enthusiastic!

While dancing the roles
they've always dreamed about,
their dancing becomes

STRONGER,

FUNNIER,

ACCEPTED!

The Trocks open minds to . . .

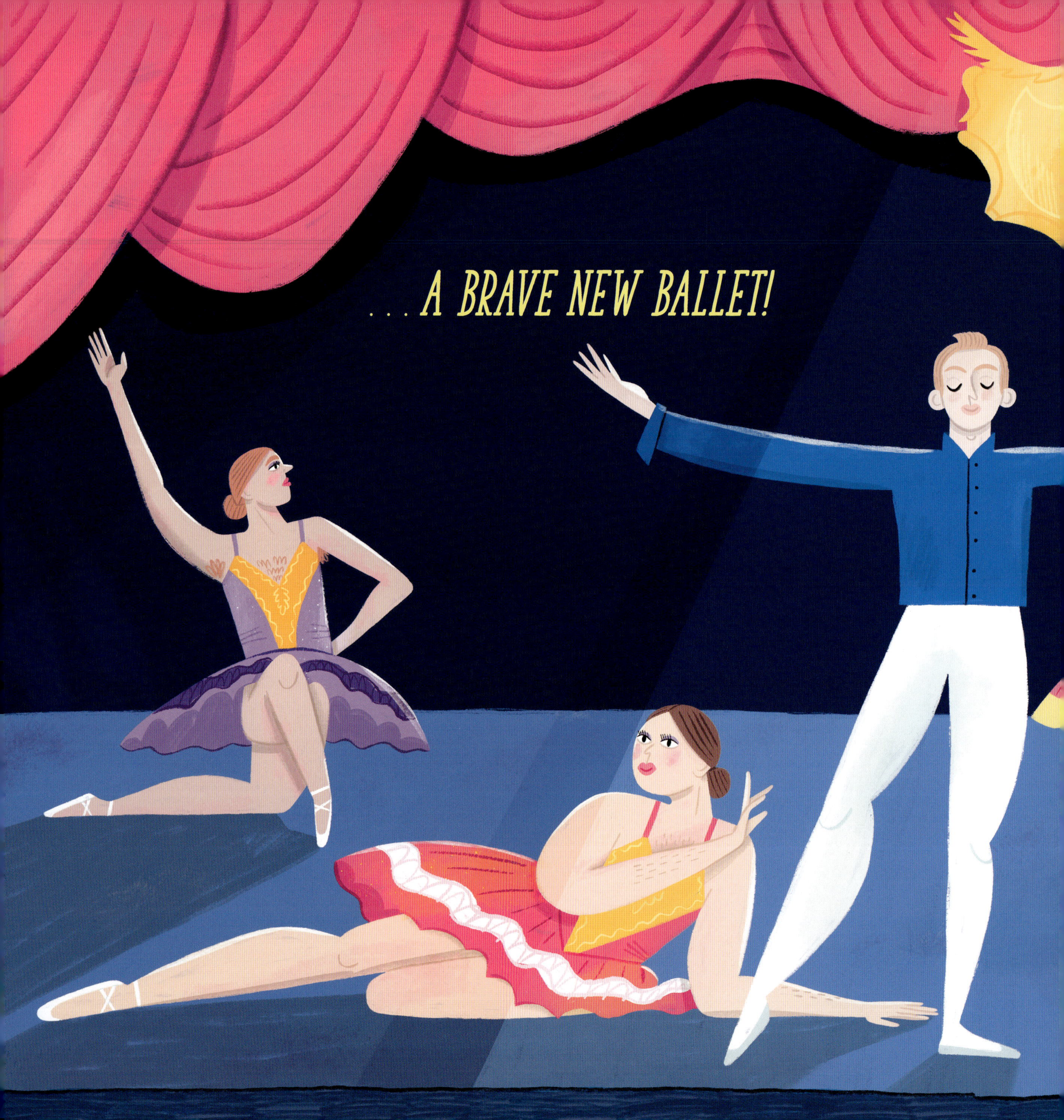
. . . A BRAVE NEW BALLET!

Finally seen as a true ballet company,
the Trockaderos take their show on tour.

From buses on country roads to airplanes around the world,
Les Ballets Trockadero de Monte Carlo
welcomes everyone!

And their dream of dancing center stage
under the bright lights?

It wasn't just a dream . . .
but a fairy tale come true.

HISTORY

In 1974, ballet, modern, and hip-hop dance companies sprang up in every corner of New York City. A group of male dancers with a background in theater wanted to dance ballet and have fun at the same time! Together, Peter Anastos, Natch Taylor, and Anthony Bassae formed a troupe with other like-minded dancers for whom traditional companies were not a perfect fit.

Taking inspiration from the great Ballets Russes, Les Ballets Trockadero de Monte Carlo was born. The Trocks combined satire and technical precision while dressing in drag. Using facial expressions and exaggerating imperfections, these dancers found the artistic freedom to be as funny as they wanted to be, all while telling a story within the story—something many of the men had not done before. The dancers found a place to belong. A troupe of their own.

The company's big break came when Arlene Croce, a dance critic for the *New Yorker*, wrote a glowing review of their performance.

"The Monte Carlo is the creation of ballet fanatics. They've seen the performances, memorized the steps, read the books (this shows in the program notes), listened to the music (this shows in the editing of the taped scores), and turned the whole scorching experience inside out," Croce wrote. Her review catapulted the Trocks to success. And in 1977, when Shirley MacLaine introduced them on national television in the United States, their once-limited audience grew exponentially!

It is important to note that travesty ballets, in which men perform male and female roles onstage as a form of parody, had been performed over a century earlier. However, in the early 1970s, the gay rights movement was just beginning, and activists demanded the right for all gay people to live openly as they wished, in safety and without discrimination. Les Ballets Trockadero de Monte Carlo helped to pave the way for freedom from traditional gender roles in the dance world.

Les Ballets Trockadero de Monte Carlo has performed in over six hundred cities and forty-three countries worldwide. For fifty years and counting, the Trocks have delighted and inspired audiences, persisting in their mission to celebrate an inclusive ballet.

AUTHOR'S NOTE

When I first saw Les Ballets Trockadero de Monte Carlo perform in Austin, Texas, I immediately fell in love. Who knew that ballet didn't have to be so serious? And that men didn't always have to save the princess but could BE the princess? I reached out to Michael McKinley, my former ballet classmate who had danced with the Trocks for over a decade. Michael shared with me his vibrant experience dancing and touring with the company. Not long after, I had the pleasure to talk with Peter Anastos, one of the founders of Les Ballets Trockadero de Monte Carlo. Peter had so much more to share about the troupe's history, the founding of the company, and the early struggles they faced.

I have a deep appreciation for all that the Trocks have accomplished—executing classical ballets with beauty, grace, and lots of laughs!

MORE ABOUT LES BALLETS TROCKADERO DE MONTE CARLO

"Ballet Legend Tory Dobrin of the Trocks." Interviews with Ballet Legends. October 27, 2023. YouTube, 57:14. https://www.youtube.com/watch?v=XJvlzfXxdHM.

Croce, Arlene. "Dancing, The Two Trockaderos." *New Yorker*. October 14, 1974, 182–188.

Gazit, Chana, and Martie Barylick, dir. *Ballerina Boys*. 2021, Merrywidow Films.

"#KnowYourTrock: Trocks Co-Founder Peter Anastos." Les Ballets Trockadero de Monte Carlo. December 10, 2020. YouTube, 33:04. https://www.youtube.com/watch?v=iZDFd8GonVg.

Les Ballets Trockadero de Monte Carlo. https://trockadero.org/.

Seitz, Jonelle. "Les Ballets Trockadero de Monte Carlo: A Peek Beneath the Tutu from Austin's Mike McKinley." *Austin Chronicle*. February 3, 2012. https://www.austinchronicle.com/arts/2012-02-03/les-ballets-trockadero-de-monte-carlo/.